POEMS FOR THE WANDERING MIND

Gene W. O'Neill

Kindle Direct Publishing

This book is dedicated to my wife, Sara O'Neill.
Her love, encouragement and kindness of spirit,
have made all of the good things in my life possible.

"To get the full value of joy you must have someone to devide it with."

"A clear conscience is the sure sign of a bad memory."

MARK TWAIN

CONTENTS

INTRODUCTION

This book is a collection of prose, blank verse and poetry. Much of the material began as poetry that sometimes evolved into song lyrics. I don't set out to create rhymes, but they end up that way if I'm anywhere near a guitar. I'll usually read the things I'm working on out loud. If it sounds funny, stupid or God forbid, profound, I'll let the rhythm of the words call the shots. Some of the material is rather old. "The Hand Wound Clock" had its start from hearing my Dad wind his clock for work. This would have been circa 1966. I was in the seventh grade. The beginning lines- "I hear tomorrow's anthem being wound," sort of popped into my head. Don't have a clue where that came from. I didn't finish that poem until recently. I enjoy the rowdy, sometimes rude mode of speech that I and many of my fellow southerners use. You'll find a fair amount of that in this book. Not unlike blues and rock lyrics, the comfortable cadence of the words are best served with bad grammar and slang. Words spoken or sung with rhythm are more pleasing to my ears.

"By The French Broad River", "Redneck Theater", and "The Seeing Eye Grocery" are sheer inventions. They contain slight references to our quaint Southern way of life. They have only lived briefly in the confined recesses of my mind. Much of the material is this book could fall under the heading of possibly successful experiments. "Seven Haikus" is my attempt at exploring a very difficult art form that appears to be simple. It is not. "Life Sonnet and "You're The Man" are my fractured attempts at exploring the sonnet form. "Go With What You Know" began as a lyric and evolved into a strange form of blank verse. "Word On the Street" attempts to convey a rough form of street life that is fading away. "The Sailors Song" and "Euphoria" are lyric songs that began as coffee house tunes written and recorded in the middle 1990's. My dear friend, David Glenn and I have performed these two songs many time through the years. "Electronic Salvation","Paradise", "Lost America", "One World" and "A Hole In the Ground" are direct observations of different aspects of current life in the United States.

Poems of a more personal nature would include: "Rusted Rabbit Blues", "Fog Dude", "Fun to Me" and "I Know I Am". Direct references to my Southern heritage should include: "High Over Head", "Clock, the Mule", "Moped Head" and "Good Lord Willing". I welcome your commentary and thank you for finding time to read these poems. I would suggest reading some of this work, or any other poem aloud. In much the same way that song lyrics 'live' when sung, poems truly come to life when spoken.

CIRCLE MAKES SPHERE

1.Square makes cube-circle makes sphere.

Sun makes light-light makes clear.

Light makes shadow-shadow makes dark.

Fire needs fuel-fuel needs spark.

2.Love needs feeling-feeling needs heart.

Heart needs passion-passion needs start.

Hope needs vision-vision needs dream.

Dream needs faith-in things unseen.

3.Dream gives purpose-purpose needs plan.

plan needs action-action needs hand.

Hands give service-service ends fear.

circle of love-circle makes sphere.

CATHOLIC SCHOOL

We lived across the street
from the church and school.

I didn't have a chance.

I could have said I didn't have a prayer.
But I had plenty of those.

Our nuns were Sisters of Saint Joseph.
Never saw them with their heads uncovered.
Never was sure they had any hair.

They wore big, clicky beads
and stern expressions.

You didn't have a chance of risking hell's fire
while they were on duty.

Those clicky beads could be wrapped in the nun's habit.
We never heard them coming.

Suddenly, the brass capped yardstick
would rain pain on the wicked.

I truly did love some of those nuns.
Some, I could not.

HIGH OVERHEAD

I'm glad that I was born in the south with my
slow southern drawl-two or more is ya'll
when it's time to go I'm liable to say:
"I'm fixing to go-got my foot in the door.*"
(*facetiously pronounced as 'doe')

Bridge: And, I guess my northern brothers
              might keep on thinking-
              we're all like Goober and the boys

Perhaps, to you I seem like some sort of
provincial lout-in a state of denial.
I equate what you bring to us
As a case of fleas,
for my cat-keep them please.

CHORUS:

High overhead-you're just a blip on a radar screen
High overhead-you're just a blip on a radar screen
the sun to your right on the morning flight
fly away-go back home

If you hear someone say: "howdy, beau."
No need to freak-that's just how we speak.
You make us wish that you're not here,
when you look down your nose-
find the thorn-miss the rose.

LOST AMERICA

Add your love-subtract your pain.
Multiply your joys-divide your gains.
Grow inside. And, do not hide,
the love you hold-don't be so cold.

And, while I am afraid of the things-
that might go wrong-I know-
this can't go on like this.

Make no vows. Swear no oaths.
Let what you do-speak for you.
And, set aside-dreams of things-
that you might control,
as you lose your soul.

A CHILD SMILES

1.Running in circles I fly to the places,

where freedom delivers and hope abides.

And, the pointless feelings we're forced to consider,

do not rule the places we're forced to stay.

And, if I was someone born clever,

I would ride the roads I'm forced to trudge.

I would be living a plan better constructed.

and, I would at least understand the pain I feel.

2.The distant and near, pleas for deliverance,

do nothing to quench the thirst I feel.

And, I wonder how anyone rises above,

the rat maze trap-we stay lost in?

Do the voices that coax us say anything?

Do the pictures that shine-give us anything to see?

Do the thumping cars that ravage our nights sleep,

have any place to go-worth going?

3.The armies are massing-to appease their makers.

Marching out to expunge-the ones unaware.

The makers of death and destruction,

hand out mirrors to reflect their views.

The children spew forth-unguided and unloved,
their parents wash their parts-and, go again.
missiles of unguided doom and plenty,
jealous of a fate they do not suspect.

4.The media makers fill our brains with wanting.
Never giving means to obtain-no, never.
Light pictures substituted for attainment,
the dreams they give-are never real.

5.A child sitting in a quiet place,
a mind that sees everything so clear.
Stands up and walks to the nearest window,
blinks and smiles-and we all disappear.

LOUIS ARMSTRONG

The cornet found the young man-
trapped in reform school.
Later, he was rescued by the trumpet,
and, from there , his sound came rolling out.
"-That cat had some good licks right away."

On the job training: played trumpet on riverboats,
in bars, gin joints and even a few whore houses.

"-Folks wanted to have some good music
when they were having a good time.
If they liked what you did, they'd ask you back.
They usually did."

His early bands, The Hot Five and The Hot Seven,
gave classes in hot jazz music.
"-Some of that stuff was so jacked up,
you could break a sweat just listening to it."
If his stuff didn't move you, you were already dead.

When he sang, you had to love him.

"-Satchmo never did worry about singing the words right.
If it swung, that's all that mattered."

When he laughed, those eyes made you smile.
"-Most everybody in the room felt like he was singing to them.
   Not everybody can do that."

DON'T PUT ME DOWN

1.

I was a challenge-You had to take

it ain't like you had a-heart I could break

If I was like those other guys

that wrecked your heart and ran

then, I could understand

CHORUS:

Don't put me down darling

Don't put me dear

2.

If time lends perspective-the Sun is next door

and, Alpha Centauri-is right down the road

The point that I am trying to make

it's just too big to grasp

and, my mind wants to explode

to CHORUS

Bridge:

Well, it ain't like I ain't been around

once, I drove a car to town

parked that car, and I watched the lights

but, I ain't never seen nothing

like you, baby, half as bright

3.

Isn't it funny? -A creepy guy like me
with a cool girl like you
I'm crushed by your silence
and, I can never be free
you can go-back to your friends
and, pretend you don't know me
but, that isn't how it was

THE STREET FESTIVAL

1.People run and dance in the street.

Grandma and baby grooving to the beat.

One just born and one just leaving.

I watch 'em both-I'm not believing.

CHORUS:

And, I'm gone-yes I'm gone.

I'll take you there if you want to go.

And, I'm gone-yes, I'm gone.

Can't plan it out or plot it out.

No, no, no, no, no.

Only Love-love-love-love love,

can take you there.

2.Play my tunes for the dancing crowd.

I try to groove-but not too loud.

Talk with folks-between my songs.

Maybe book a job-don't run too long.

3.They take your card and never call you.

If you could not laugh-it might just gall you.

It's a silly game-you have to laugh.

They steal your soap-then say you need a bath.

CLOCK, THE MULE

Clock, the mule-Clock, the mule.
Wouldn't take nothing for Clock, the mule.
Right on time-'most all the time.
That old mule-had a working mind.
Snaked out logs for Grandpa's mill.
(Got places a tractor couldn't go.)

Folks kept mules for all sorts of chores.
For plowing and hauling most anything.
If you didn't have money for a tractor,
you might have the means to get a mule.

Grandaddy told me-that mule could tell time.
Clock always knew: the time to rest,
the time to work-the time eat,
and-when we ought to go home.
Sometimes-he'd quit when he felt like it.
He'd do no more work that day.
(And, that was that.)

ELECTRONIC SALVATION

1.I know Jesus ain't in heaven,
he's walking 'round down here
taking names-checking out all
the fools on the PC-acting like
they're prophets on the take.
Well, I guess that just proves-
that the product must be good,
to survive they're handling.
No, I won't attend your church
it's still too small CHORUS

Chorus:
Religion-television-politicians with guns
contrition and attrition,
looking out for number one.
 All about number one.

2.I don't watch my television-too much anymore.

I got tired of all the crap

they've been shoveling.

dark fantasies that seldom-bring us hope.

Their hungers and their pains,

seep into our brains;

and, leave us thinking:

hope's replacement needs-

a plasma screen-how obscene.

CHORUS

> Turn off your TV-shut down your PC
>
> find any excuse-to get away

3.I went to the art museum-

saw all that stuff in there,

all laid out-all prepared

in advance of some future.

It made me wonder-if someday,

in some distant, undreamed land,

some guy like me would stand-

in silent wonder:

the TV must have been a sacred shrine

they worshiped all the time

CHORUS

THE SEEING EYE GROCERY

1.I'm going down to the liquor store.
   running low and I want some more.
   Drank until I hit the floor.
   Better not go to the liquor store.

2.Or, maybe I'll go to The Seeing Eye.
   Get some grits and ham for me to fry.
   Eating that stuff 'll make you die.
   Better not go to The Seeing Eye.

3.Or, maybe I will check the mail.
   Ain't no telling what's on sale.
   I hear Rodney's out on bail.
   Maybe, I won't check the mail.

4.I really ought to take a bath.
  'Smell kind of bad-don't you laugh.
   My water bill's been cut in half.
   I don't guess I'll take a bath.

5.I'm going down to the liquor store.
   Then, get grits and ham like before.
   Take a bath and sweep the floor.
   But first I'm going to the liquor store.

HAND WOUND CLOCK

I hear tomorrow's anthem being wound,
an even metered sound.
Constant as the ocean,
deafening with it's roar.
Disturbing restful dreams,
marking, making chores.
Sonic grid to guide the masses,
clicks and ticks-for time that passes.
on we trudge-still indebted,
don't you dare-forget to set it.

TRUCK STOP COFFEE

With a pound of sugar and a pint of cream,
you're a coffee lover's kind of dream.
The kind of stuff that'll keep you up-
for more than a day.
Makes your G.I. tract act in funny ways.

   My Doc told me I'd have to make some changes-
   in my crazy life:
   quit being married-or quit drinking coffee.
   How am I going to tell my wife?

With a pound of sugar and a pint of cream,
you're a coffee lover's kind of dream.
black as night-like India ink,
that's the swill I love to drink.

LIFE SONNET

Who says life is fair? No one that I know
The process moves on. It has no feeling.
Raging stream unchecked. Going where it will.
You, go with the flow. Ignore the peril.

You drown with great haste. We witness this waste.
No scale to measure. No weight to be weighed.
The sum of living: no number to count.
Seen in abstraction. A puzzle unsolved.

Time of great knowing: so does it exist?
So what do we seek? Pleasant interludes?
High places unclimbed? Better songs to sing?
Beautiful bodies? Work that has meaning?

Peers that respect us? Sorrow left unknown?
There is no resting, only what comes next.
No bridge to wisdom, no gold to buy truth.
Seeing that you see-joy without price tags.

BABY DOLLS AND PARTY GIRLS

1.I don't like to work, no sir.

   I'd rather drink and dance.

   the only time I want to sweat,

   is when I make romance.

   I'm a randy, dandy ne'er–do–well,

   with my pompadour and cane.

   Only one thing on my mind,

   I got a party on the brain.

CHORUS: I love those baby dolls

       and those party girls,

       baby dolls and those party girls.

       I can't wait to see my baby doll.

2.I remember ole Miss Beale,

   rocking on her porch.

   I heard she was a flapper gal,

   that never held a torch.

   She drank and danced and messed around,

   her family was disgraced.

Died in her sleep at ninety-two-
with a big smile on her face.

3.Joan and Connie have a life,
filled with love and light.
They're not concerned with your ideas,
of what is wrong or right.
Love binds them together,
that's all they need to know.
I'm proud to call 'em friends,
and watch their kids grow.

MOPED HEAD

I'm a silly hillbilly with a city boy toy
I play too loud, but I like the noise
I'm Ernest Tubb, bub-with a be-bop doo
a swivel hip trip with an attitude

I got a moped head with a Cadillac heart
ain't too slick, but, I'm kind of smart
want to take it real slow-I can do my part
I got a moped head-with a Cadillac heart

Made a love shack, baby-in the back of my car
got some lightning bugs in an ole fruit jar
let the bugs go while we're making love
we're floating along with the stars above

I got a moped head with a Cadillac heart
ain't too slick, but, I'm kind of smart
want to take it real slow-I can do my part
I got a moped head-with a Cadillac heart

GENE W. O'NEILL

24

Made a buttercup crown for you that day
we kept it 'til it fell away
sipped honeysuckle, baby-right from the vine
them honey bees didn't seem to mind.

PARADISE

Do you ever wake up in the morning
And, wonder if-this'll be the day that it happens?
When the reasons run out for playing the game-
Lord knows-some people give up;
And live with their eyes half-closed
The PC guides lead 'em 'round by the nose.
Mistaking apathy- for peace of mind.

Sometimes it seems kind of foolish-
Going through the motions-for no reason.
While the question still remains,
Will it ever change?
And will we ever make it to Paradise?
Is Paradise more than a dream?
Will we ever make it to Paradise?
Is Paradise-more than a dream?

You try to keep things in perspective
But how do you do it when the picture-keeps on changing?
You try to live your life one day at a time,
while racing the engines of doom into tomorrow.

While the question still remains,
Will it ever change?
Will we ever make it to Paradise?
Is Paradise more than a dream?

A HOLE IN THE GROUND

I'm no witness for insanity-
I'd rather do right and let the
other guy be.
Jump up cussing-
you better sit right down,
can't do no living in a hole in the ground.

Gotta do right-and, get the word around
can't do living-can't do no living
can't do no living-
in a hole in the ground

A roach motel ain't a baby's toy,
Mama needs Daddy for-
the girls and boys.
A little kid shouldn't have
a mean, hard face,
turn off that TV and
take 'em some place.

You say, Good Lord! It's

a crying shame.

quit talking like that-

'cause we're all to blame.

Kids learn about killing

on that ol' TV,

hope they don't want to practice on me.

WITTY, CLEVER AND SMART

Witty, Clever and Smart,
met a quandary of the mind.
Each with a mode of action,
each path-vaguely defined.
Witty made remarks with humor,
with no plans to share.
Clever implied many things,
with no fruits to bear.
Smart remained in silence,
leaving quandary in despair.
Witty, Clever and Smart,
partners in a crime.
Left quandary searching,
for a better paradigm.

ANY WAR

Far away, laying in a shallow grave-
are the remains of someone's child.
Gone to war. Gone to war.
Who still remembers-
what were they fighting for?
It seemed important. So important.
So important then.

Stone monuments, flags and speeches,
stirring tributes for those that died.
How freedom was in danger,
Yet, freedom remains denied.
Their wars begin with subterfuge.
greed and hate-built with careful lies.

No need to study reason,
no need to know a name.
No need to find the truth,
We simply shift the blame.

GENE'S ZOO

1. I'm an old gray tabby and I rule the house,
   don't expect me-to chase your mouse.
   I'll crap in the box and puke on the floor,
   like I've done many times before.

2. I'm a squirrel in the yard-I chase the birds,
   steal all their food-it's so absurd.
   The neighbor's dog's life is hard,
   loses his blues by going in my yard.

3. I'm an ant-with a million friends,
   Seems like the swarms will never end.
   we'll set up shop and fight to stay.
   give us ant acid and we'll freak away.

4. I'm a sweet old possum-I make no fuss,
   can't figure why folks are scared of us.
   we don't tote guns-we don't sell drugs,
   we don't get rabies-and we eat bad bugs.

5. I'm a displaced deer-I'm a refugee,
   there is no place nearby for me.
   Bed in tall grass in the neighborhood,
   things for us-aren't looking so good.

6.I'm a little bird-sitting in a tree,
   I see the world-looking back at me.
   It really doesn't matter who you are,
   glad to be the bird-that craps on your car.

REDNECK THEATER

1.Tommy took a ride to Bennie's.
   Bennie had some dope for Joy.
   But Joy didn't have much money.
   So, Bennie went and got annoyed.
   Joy said: "I'd better call Billy."
   Billy said: "You need to talk to Roy."
   But Roy wasn't home that day,
   he was probably out with the boys.

2.Billy left to see Patty.
   Patty was a local cop.
   Joy knew right then, best thing to do,
   was let the matter drop.

3.Well, Tommy was still at Bennie's,
   and, he started taking up for Joy.
   He said: "I'll be glad to split that bag-
   there ain't no need to bother Roy."

4.Roy had fallen from his tree stand.
  Pink Davis had found him dead.
  It seems Bennie had sold Roy something-
  that knocked him out of his head.

  5.Pink never did like Roy,
didn't mind that Roy was dead.
Roy was a hateful talking man,
swore 'most every word he said.

6."I reckon I'll call Patty,
   his daughter would want to know."
  When Pink tried to call her-
  he found out she wasn't home.

7.Her shift had already started,
  she was on patrol that night.
  She had the strangest feeling,
  something-something wasn't right.

8.Before they knew it-it was time to do it,
Roy was laying at the funeral hall.
The folks that loved and hated him,
said "The big man sure looks small."

9.Roy looked funny wearing a suit-
Where was that smelly ol' cigar?
Bennie skipped the visitation-
and headed straight to the bar.

10.A ragged procession-began to fill the room.
A tawdry fragrance slowly wafted:
brown liquor and cheap perfume.
Pink looked a little too happy,
Joy looked a little too high.
Looked like Patty couldn't decide,
if she was going to laugh or cry.

11.Soon it was decided: an impromptu celebration!
A free bar was promised-guaranteeing
participation.
Folks suddenly recalled-their deep love for Roy.
The promise of a better buzz-sounded good to Joy.

12.They all adjourned-to the local bar-
to drink and reminisce.
Bennie shouted: "I don't like the look of this!
Ya'll can't prove nothing. I wasn't even there."
Pink says: "Shut the hell up! Don't nobody care."

(It seems as though-more than a few did care.)

Eyewitnesses later stated:

"Benine finished his drink-staggered out the door. After that night-the dealer was seen no more. A bad ending resulted from deals he had made. He left the world friendless,his bar tab still unpaid."

SEVEN HAIKUS

1.

The moon bids farewell
birds sing to greet the dawning
The morning beckons

2.

Our fear seeks darkness
as the shadows fear the sun
wisdom brings the light

3.

Children see the world
and try to search for meaning
old folks do the same

4.

Fish breaths in water
and it drowns when breathing air
we live where we can

5.

A small rock can hurt
when it's trapped inside a shoe
Shoes on rock-no pain

6.

Glad to be alive
many do not know this joy
kindness must be shared

7.

Hills are there to climb
The valleys try to hold us
courage makes us try

SQUARED AWAY MARINE

I ran and shot and killed today.
Paris Island's far away.
I load my gun and I keep it clean.
'cause I'm a squared away Marine.

CHORUS: I'm a squared away Marine-
     I come from Idaho.
     I'm a squared away Marine-
     everywhere I go.

2.Sargent Carter-we're OK.
 Gomer Pyle ain't here today.
 The Corps ain't never had his kind.
 I may be dumb-but, I ain't blind.
 CHORUS

3.Load the ship-and, away we go.
 I don't want to miss the show.
 We kill with noise-and, we kill with stealth.
 This kind of work ain't good for your health.
 CHORUS

SOLO PERFORMER

When you play music as a solo performer,
It's all on you.
Sort of like a rodeo rider.
Once they open the gate,
it's all on you.

When everything goes good, nothing like it.
You better be ready.
You better know what you're doing.
And you better have a plan b, c and d,
for when things go wrong.

Weddings are hardly ever fun.
Receptions almost always are.
Restaurants and gallery showings
are my favorites.

When folks recognize my talent,
such as it is-
they'll respect me

and leave me to do what I do.

I play a lot of jazz, blues, 60's soul and
some country, done with a little swing.
Classical only for weddings.
Nothing, but nothing from the 21st century.

You spend a fair amount of time keeping
your instruments in tune.
Once the music starts, tuning becomes difficult.

I'll switch back and forth between
the nylon string and the jazz box.
That little bit of contrast helps a lot.
The fingers don't mind either.

Most of my repertoire
means nothing
to the young folks.
I'm okay with that.

Sometimes they'll listen long enough
to decide they like it.

COMPANY MAN

Lost a few fingers on the line-
the OSHA man never seems to mind.
The boys upstairs just pay the fine-
I might not be so lucky next time.

The boss says jump- and I ask how high,
don't even bother asking why.
I'm never sick and I'm never late,
and when the rumors start-I set 'em straight.

CHORUS:
I'm a company man-I love the job I do,
I'm a company man- I see things through.
I walk the chalk line when the big boys draw it,
if they told me to-I'd even crawl it.

I'm just one of the boys-one of the crew,
don't mind being told what to do.
Thrifty, loyal, brave and true,
a boy scout at 62.

'Times I lie awake at night-
think about things done wrong and right.
and, how I worked the job too long,
while my dreams still lingered on. CHORUS.

BY THE FRENCH BROAD RIVER

1.I went for a walk-down by the French Broad River.

A cat walked up to me.

Instead of saying 'meow',

He began speaking French.

"Cat, you can't be doing that!"

He replied: "Relax, son.

I'm just practicing my French."

"What makes you think-I speak any French ?" I said.

2.He says: "Lookey here,Son.

We're down here-by The French Broad River.

So everybody here-ought to speak French!"

But I explained: "I don't live around here."

Cat says: "Okay, I guess that'll have to do.

Son, by the way, since we're friends,

could you get me some nourriture?

That's French for vittles," he explained.

3.He followed me back-to my beat-up Honda.

That's when I found-I'd locked my keys in the car.

The cat says "-Don't freak; son-

you've got that spare in your wallet."

A talking cat with e.s.p.? That might come in handy.

After we shared my lunch,

I started thinking out loud:

"Cat, what do you think about

coming home with me?"

Cat says: "That might be all right.

Let me think about it."

4.The very next day-I was headed for home,

the cat was sitting there next to me.

No one said anything for the longest time.

Cat says: "Son, I'm willing to give this a try."

I said: "Good deal. Let's see what happens."

5.Everything was pretty smooth-

I was glad for the company.

That cat and I were doing fine,

'til I got home one day-checked my phone bill.

I thought that I'd flip my lid.

"Hey cat! Who do you know in Paris, France?"

6.Cat says: "How can I improve my French unless-

I'm talking to people that speak French?"

I said: "They've got folks in New Orleans

that speak French.

I can pay for THAT phone bill!"

He said: "I KNOW that, Son.

But, I want the real thing!"

7."Well, la-di-dah!" I said.

"You're going to have to get a job."

Cat doesn't miss a beat.

Cat says: "I figure we can clean up gambling."

I'm thinking: "Yes! He could read

the other players' minds."

The cat says: "No-no. They won't let cats in there!

They'd say it was bad luck!

We could go to the track-no one would even care.

They've got a good horse track in New Orleans.

I speak fluent horse,

which is a lot like mule, but faster.

You could get rich and my French

would be très bien."

FUN TO ME

1.My Mama told me I'd let her down.

Instead of going to church-I'd go to town.

Watched the drunks and whores make the rounds.

Looked like fun to me.

2.My Daddy said son -"Can't you be like me?"

Play sports on courts-hit balls off tees?

But, a guitar was all that I could see.

Looked like fun to me.

3.Strange that folks that didn't have a clue,

wanted to tell me what to do.

All that crap they'd put you through,

was no fun to me.

4.Blues and country music spoke to me.

A stylized form of reality.

Sing about things that use to be.

Sounds like fun to me.

5.Now, the little kids-ain't kids no more.

Pick up licks from the iTunes store.

Make my jaw drop to the floor.

Looks like fun to me.

6.Now, lawyers and voyeurs infest this life.

Fanning the flames of doubt and strife.

all too glad to sell you the knife.

That ain't no fun to me.

7.Hope I ain't here when the hammer falls.

Man with the plan-gets kicked in the balls.

Greedy, grid lock devils-swept from the halls.

Sounds like fun to me.

ONE WORLD

There's 'plenty good people left in the world-
bad guys just get-all the attention.
You can holler for help or call the police-
but don't expect divine intervention.

With everybody looking out for number one,
I think it's time the victims started having fun.
Isn't this one world- for everyone?
A dream worth coming true-
but not for me and you.
Isn't this one world-for everyone?
One world-One world starting today.

I believe in tact and manners;
and, it's sweet seeing people when they
try to be kind.

you don't have to lower the boom
every time-that you're able-
just 'cause the boys on the street-
don't deal in tact and manners.

Well, I only believe half of what I read,
'cause, the internet mostly deals in ratings.
They'll sell more add space to the dead-
the kind of folks that live off of hating.

FATHER, SON AND THE HOLY GHOST

I died last night in my sleep you know,
the only part left of me-
got up and went work as usual,
'was running late so I skipped the funeral.

I'm man who's covered from head to toe
with mirrors that reflect your views.
you see, my thoughts-they're all second hand,
can't play the game-I'm still in the stands.

Father, Son and Holy Ghost,
Oh, I'm needing you the most.
And, I need you now.
Father, Son and Holy Ghost,
Going out from coast to coast.

GENE   W. O'NEILL

I can't wait around for judgment day,

I'd better get a better plan.

I gotta move-gotta get going,

yeh, my worry streak is showing.

Now, what if all those holy books-

ain't nothing but a stack of lies?

I wonder if anyone would notice-

if they all said-"you're the one that wrote us."

FOG DUDE

1.There I go-staring out the window again.
   There I go-acting like a dream is a friend.

Bridge: Sometime I think that I'm insane-
          chasing dreams and fleeing pain.
          I may be crazy but I get along-
          I get to choose when I-end my song.

CHORUS: You may call me-Fog Dude.
          I fly my plane at a different altitude.
          Just 'cause I'm vague-
          It don't mean I'm rude.
          I'm just a happy old-Fog Dude.

2. There I go-broken bird-'a lost in the wind.
   There I go-never, ever learning to win.

3.There I go-making like a dog on a bone.
   There I go-thinking I can make it alone.

   Repeat bridge and chorus.

IT AIN'T AS LONG AS IT HAS BEEN

It ain't as long as it has been,

on the jagged road to was and when.

Kept making choices-while all those voices,

kept telling me-what I ought to do.

But, I have made it-a lifelong quest,

to ignore the witty folk that test;

test my resolve-

while pissing on my dreams.

Complex choices-and, chances taken.

Godless youth-spawn forsaken.

Covered head to toe-with I don't know,

while pretending that they do.

That sums me in my youth,

rowdy, restless and, yes: uncouth.

An ounce of cool for a pound of pain,

I reckon I ain't doing that again.

ROCKET TO THE MOON

1.Monsieur LeBlanc has a real dilemma,

He has a mistress, and her name is Emma.

Madame LeBlanc has no sense of humor,

She got the facts once she heard the rumor.

Their divorce cost him millions of francs,

Took all the money that he had in the bank.

Madame hired someone to bump him off,

Now he's up with Emma hiding out in a loft.

He'd love to get away. In a...

Rocket to the Moon. Rocket to the Moon.

2.Doctor Bob is a plastic surgeon,

Money makes beauty-that's his conversion.

His wife shops on Rodeo Drive,

it's good to be king-good to be alive.

He's got this lingering doubt in his mind,

was it eight sponges-well, it could have been nine.

Then, the lawyers started knocking on his door,

now, he can't do those tummy tucks no more.

He'd love to get away. In a...

Rocket to the Moon. Rocket to the Moon.

Like to get away-cannot stay-

can't wait for another day.

3.Anne makes her money as a yuppie dog walker,

Pretty smile and a real smooth talker.

They all love Anne-and, they don't know why.

When she gets home-she will meditate,

chants and prays and she will not hate.

Stand next to her and you feel the good,

I'd go where she goes-if I only could.

I'd like to get away. In a...

Rocket to the Moon. Rocket to the Moon.

Like to get away-cannot stay-

can't wait for another day.

CALL THE SHOTS

1.How'd we ever get in this-situation
   out of the frying pan and into the fire
   I remember when you called me-honey baby
   now all you ever call me-is a liar.

   You can call the shots-I don't mind.
   You can call the shots-all right okay.
   You can call the shots-ain't going to worry.
   You can call the shots-all right okay.

2.I guess you'd say we're a bad combination
   fire and ice-water and oil and such
   still, it all blends together-oh so nicely
   all it takes-is that loving touch

   You can call the shots-I don't mind.
   You can call the shots-all right okay.
   You can call the shots-ain't going to worry.
   You can call the shots-all right okay.

3.Now if you can find a better way-to do this
I'm all ears-baby let me know.
Just 'cause someone gets all angry
doesn't mean someone has to go.

BAILEY

Bailey don't have anyone to take her home
she's much too busy working at her job
she's actively committed to a better world
secretly, she like be in love

CHORUS:
Bailey, you're not dealing with the hunger
That should not matter-often times it does
You deserve better than you're doing
I know-love will find
love will find-love will find-your door
How many people in this world
are just like you-sweet, solitary people
that would love to love you

Bailey don't need anyone to wreck her house
she'd just have to clean it up again
The status quo walks the wire in silence
  if you can't take a lover-take a friend

HEAD OVER HEELS

There are 12 windows in my little house
that let the light in to my sweet spouse
there're 17 steps in my little place
I'd run up each one to touch her face

CHORUS: Head over heels and heart over mind
        lucky for me that love is blind
        love so real and it's right on time
        love so real and it's right
        right on time

They say carbon 30 atoms bounce like hell
they quit making Superballs
so, I'll never tell
Loving you baby's, like playing on
a trampoline-
except I keep my change
and, I stay real clean (Chorus)

Now if you're on the Eiffel Tower

you're in Paris, France

when I think about you, baby-

I want to be in your pants

that rude and it's crude

sometimes I'm crass

but love like yours

is hard to pass   (Chorus)

GOOD LORD WILLING

Checks in the mail and I know I owe,
in one hand and out it goes.
money's all gone, and I don't know where-
reckon I'll work in my rocking chair.

A poor man's life is an uphill climb.
You pay your dues, and you bide your time.
Work all day 'til the sun goes down.
Get back up when the work bell sounds

Good Lord willing and the creek don't rise.
A man is born, and a man will die.
Dogs 'll bark and birds 'll fly.
Good lord willing and the creek don't rise.

I NEVER CAUGHT THE TRAIN

1. I've chased your ghost,
   for the longest time.
   Stopped my hopes and dreams,
   parked 'em on a dime.
   The times together,
   made it worth the pain.
   I chased your memory,
   but I never caught the train.

2. Long nights-feeling empty,
   hung by memory rope.
   Drank for distraction,
   I never learned to cope.
   So I let my mind wander,
   blamed your past in vain.
   Found my way back,
   But I never caught the train.

3.Folks are glad to tell me,
   things I should have done.
   Traded hopes for sorrow,
    swore I was having fun.
   That dark depression,
   wanted me insane.
   I finally worked it out,
   But I never caught the train.

RUSTED RABBIT BLUES

Rusted rabbit-sitting there
right outside my door
sat there 'til he rusted
now he can't move no more

        Time goes by-good friends die
        and the criminals get away
        crime must pay-it must pay
        Don't take too long-
        to move along-and tell the tale

Rusted rabbit-keeps the spot
my dear wife put him in
I wonder if-I'm like him
does love keep you bound within?

I do for her what I would not do

for another living soul

is that control-brought by love?

Don't take too long

got to move along-and tell the tale

I can say you-you know me

I think that I-I might know you

I'm glad to say-that it works that way

That rabbit will not run today

That rabbit will not run-run away

CRAWL

Before we run we have to walk
before walk we have to stand
before we stand-before we stand
we have to crawl

1) If I could laugh-I wouldn't have to cry.
   If I was like, real smart-I would know why:
   The very things you need to know-
   are what you're never told.
   Why it's sad watching love-
   when it's growing cold.

CHORUS: If I could crawl-then, I could have you.
        If I could crawl-then, I could have you.

2) Now, look at that baby-playing on the floor.
   can't stay still-and got to move some more.
   Baby don't know-where he has to go-
   he just has to go.
   One day that baby stands right up

    and walks on out the door.

    While mama says: "Baby don't go-

    baby don't go-mama needs you still". CHORUS

3) Now, I could tell you-everything's alright.

    thought about it-over half the night,

    I decree that you and me-don't have to be a pair,

    if you can't take the kind of pain-lovers have

    to share.

DURHAM

It's still known as The Bull City.
It had lots of booze and blues-
and textile mills.
But it was tobacco that reigned supreme.
Bull Durham. Ligget and Myers. American Tobacco.
Ol' Buck Duke helped to found a university.
You may have heard about that.

Working folks had a dream
to get a job at the factories.
But all those jobs-they went away.
Trendy shops and restaurants
occupy a space still haunted
by the scent of tobacco long gone.

if you come to Durham-you're going to see,
the all-pervading influence-of Duke University.
If you're sick-they'll try to make you well.
If you've got the grades and the money,
you can get everything they have for sell.

To see the sights-you might go downtown,
giant cranes seem to pull
those buildings from the ground.
In place of creeping urban blight,
you'll hunt for a parking place at night.

YOU GO WITH WHAT YOU KNOW

The past is a story-you keep on retelling
it changes a little-each time it's told
I wonder how many-
of the truths that we lean on,
deserve much more than a smile and a flush?
You go with what you know.

I can't conceive of this pagan insanity
religion of commerce that rules one and all
Run to your PC-craving humanity
nothing's on Facebook-a big waste of time
You go with what you know.

This fantasy life-that I have been living
is very fulfilling-except when it sucks
So what am I trying-to say at this moment
I'm just killing time-like they do with the news.
You go with what you know.

I have to admit that sometimes I am gullible
I'd rather believe you-given the choice
But I have some friends that cannot bear mendacity
they lock up their hearts-as they run you away
You go with what you know.

DON'T WANT TO BE LIKE YOU

I ain't got lots of money
don't drive no fancy car
It's too cloudy most of the time
for me to wish on a star

But, I get a lovely feeling
when I'm doing what I can do
free as a bird-flying above the heard
I don't want to be...
Don't want to be like you

I'm too lazy to be happy
I'm too blue to keep joy
don't guess I'm gonna grow up
reckon I'll be a good old boy

But, I guess I've done all right
done what I've wanted to do
free to be-free to see
I don't want to be...
Don't want to be like you

Ain't saying no one's better
That ain't like me
But, when my sound is flowing out
it sets my sad soul free

YOU'RE THE MAN (SONNET)

A mind awakens-seeing worlds unseen
two lands: is and will be-lost in between.
The mind sets a quest-did not know it craved.
Reason flowing in-logic is enslaved.

Point That brain-like a gun at the problem.
This thing will never slow you down.
Aching to show it who's boss-who pays the cost,
when you have no time to doubt.
Show 'em how it's done. You're the man.

Burning search begins-
with peace of mind no more.
Pounding on minds door-
bloody hands implore:
"The answer-the answer-what shall it be?"
The mind rages onward-"why can't you see?"
Vortex of knowledge-spins dark in the night.

A spiral-a spin-the brain-a notion of light?
Drink ever deeper-from false hope and guile,
when, thoughts of substance-
have caused me to smile.

I see the course before me-plans are made.
The raging madness-slowly starts to fade.
This hunger can make the heart and soul blind,
no substitute for-simple peace of mind.

WORD ON THE STREET

1.You can see 'em selling papers
every few blocks
got a metal fold up chair-
and a couple 'big rocks.
Brave the wind, the snow and the rain,
making a living sure can get strange.

CHORUS: and, they just want something-
to make 'em feel good-
want their little piece of Hollywood.
But, their hope is a rope-
that cannot swing.
Their love is a bird that cannot sing-
it cannot sing.

2.Smooth Groove is running
his same old line.
But, his main man, Bill-
ain't buying this time
He said "-I'll get you some money-
just as soon as I can.
But, Bill ain't in the mood to understand,
talks about dusting Groove off-
with a two by four. CHORUS

3.Mary's a blank-eyed girl

that lives on the street.

She'd rather do junk-

than sleep or eat.

She wants to go home-

but she don't know how.

Her friends would not-

recognize her now. CHORUS

IS IT WORTH IT?

Pick me up-and, roll me over,
there's no crime-in growing older.
no matter what you do-
the changes-they will come.

There's no need-to rush and hurry,
 jump the gun-and, just plain worry
no matter what you do-
the changes-they will come.

I remember when we were young:
I'd pick a flower
and, you'd get stung
time brought the changes
I went along
played for the money
instead of the song
But there is no job worth your sanity
You trade your life
and your love for security
Is it worth it? Is it worth it?
I don't know

GENE W. O'NEILL

Now, I dream
of those good old days
worth so much more
than we got paid

IN THE MIX (SONG LYRIC)

1.

It took a little bit longer

than I wanted to baby,

I took it out to sea

and, I joined the Navy.

Sailed around the world

past the Cape of Good Hope,

Got hooked on a gal,

that was hooked on dope.

Junk took her life

and, my love away,

found that dealer in death

and, I blew him away.

I was In The Mix

2.

Well, the law didn't see

my point of view,

hung me as killer

for my just dues.

I waited a while

came back as a cat,

got fat as a hog

killing old wharf rats.
One day I met a rat
a little bigger than me,
and he grinned a grin
and, swallowed me.
I was in the mix.

3.
So, I became rat bait
'cause I couldn't cope,
came back again
as ol' hemp rope.
Got rolled up
in a big, fat spleaf,
and a Rasta man stuck me
between his teeth.
lit me up like a lightning rod,
and, both of us went off
to see God.
I was in the mix.

PRAYER TO WORLD

This song is my prayer to the world,

the heart's church bell calls to me.

Perhaps the holy spirit of the world,

lay in each person's mind.

Why speak to me of pearly gates,

Or streets that are covered with gold?

For these metaphors have little to do

with the greater truths-we've yet to live.

When we're awake-we're really half-asleep,

when we're afraid-we're really half alive.

when we're angry-this dark dream only brings us pain.

The world today-has gone insane,

nothing seems to matter anymore.

If we all hold on-right or wrong

then what will there be left of us to save?

Isn't it madness-to fight when it's wrong?

Isn't it madness?-The weak and the strong,

we'll all share a fate-consumed by our rage.

Isn't it madness?

Is it the world-that-breaks our hearts?
Are we too lazy to do anything-
but, gripe and moan?

Is it the past-that-rules our fate?
Safer in sorrow-than risking
a better fate unknown?

I'd really like to know.
I'd really hope to know.
I'd really want to know.

This song is my prayer to the world,
a choice-for the awakened heart to make.
The clear light sought for guidance,
only found-by honest introspection.

THE SAILORS SONG

1.All ashore -that's going ashore.
   You're going where a deck is a floor.
   Go port lane cruising-after a while-
   to hold and roll in love-love in style.

2. All ashore that's going ashore-
    I think I love you-but I need more.
    You see those blue-ocean waves?
    they're the cradle-of my dreams.

   BRIDGE: Now, for every smile that I have ever-
           put upon your face.
           Don't ever let a single doubt-
           come to take my place.

3.All ashore-that's going ashore
    Don't know what we're heading for.
    I try to steer and you say "-hard about!"
    I try to whisper-but all you want to do-
    all you want to do is shout.
    Repeat BRIDGE

    Yo-ho-ho and a bottle of rum
    I don't know where love comes from
    Men and ships going down the sea
    Took my life ad my love from me
    Away!   Away!
    (Sung as a round)

BEAUTIFUL

Chorus: You want to be beautiful.

       You want to be radiant.

       You want to be heaven sent.

       The goddess: new millennium.

       Gotta get your makeup right.

       Time for you to realize.

       The pretty girl wins the prize.

       It happens all the time.

       You want to be beautiful.

1. Why do you let people-tell you how you feel?
   The dreams they're selling-they are not real.
   We all crave attention-that much is true.
   but, the world can't help-help but, notice you.
   CHORUS

2.She said: plain is a stain-you can't wash away.
   You trade on your looks-more than what you say.
   No one will recall the clever things you've said-
   if you don't how-how to turn their head.

CHORUS

3. She said: I get what you're saying-
   but that doesn't work for me.
   I know what I want-what I want to be
   Stay slave to the "good look" if you want to be free.
That's how it works-that's plain enough for me.
CHORUS

I KNOW I AM

1.When I was just five-I found my stalk in the night,

   I didn't know what I was doing-but, it sure felt right.

   And I was lost-oh yeah-in the night.

   When I was seventeen-a girl black as the night,

    gave me her body so warm and right.

   I was lost-oh yeah- lost in the night.

   And, I don't know-when life begins,

   and, I don't know if I care.

   But, if matter can't be destroyed-

   how can it end?

   Another dream projection-

   on the screen of life-

   I know I am.

2.When I was twenty-four my woman reeled me in,

   we were lost in the love and the tales we would spin.

   we kept the cold-away from our door.

   When she found me I was playing in a band,

   no bars-no breaks-no one nightstands.

   All gone in a flash.

EUPHORIA

I ain't going to second guess myself,
Out of loving you this time.
Going to keep my mouth closed,
I'll pretend that I'm a mime.
(It works better when I do.)

Euphoria- oh I'm up and in the clouds
Euphoria- makes me want to laugh out loud
Euphoria- one and one is making two
Euphoria:-I want to play for you

I ain't going to feel sick or worried,
over you loving me.
Going to let my mind go,
Shut it down and let it be.

IT ALL COMES OUT IN MY SONG

1)I live my life on feeling
Sometimes that's right or wrong
don't know how I got like this
it all comes out in my song

2)I really like watching people
   been like this all along
   I don't understand half of what we do,
   it all comes out in my song
Where's it going to go?
if I like the song-I put it in the show,
If you like the ride-that's the way you go.

3)Sometimes I'm kind of edgy
   bounce like an old ping pong
   I don't like being the way I am
   it all comes out in my song

4)Sometimes I'm a scared little monkey
   sometimes I'm like King Kong
   it all depends on the mood I'm in
   it all comes out in my song

ABOUT THE AUTHOR

Gene W. O'neill

Gene O'Neill is the byproduct of a County Kerry Irishman and a High Point, North Carolina gal. His parents met while they were both in the Army during World War Two. Gene was the last of four children born to his family. Fearing things could only get worse, his parents gave up further efforts towards procreation. Attending at least one new school each year until graduating from High School, Gene perfected his status as a lifelong introvert. Writing became a lifelong obsession. Short stories, poetry, and letter writing became a constant. Along the way, he began playing the guitar. Soon, came a series of garage bands. This culminated in him playing professionally in several above average cover bands. While still playing professionally, He married his wonderful wife, Sara. Long phone calls and the occasional visit home were not found to be conducive to a stable marriage. Gene wisely chose to find a source of income that would allow his marriage to prosper. The author discovered the altogether unmusical trade of sheet metal fabrication. From this, a transition to a career as a machinist came next. During this time Gene enjoyed stints playing in weekend bands.

After this, he focused exclusively on playing solo guitar. Frequent music jobs resulted. During this period, Gene produced and released 5 CD's of jazz and classical guitar music. Playing weddings, jazz and blues gigs prepared him for an ongoing 20+ year gig at The Irregardless Café in Raleigh, North Carolina. The author continued to work as a machinist until his retirement in 2020. From this time onward, his marriage, writing and music have remained the center of Gene's world.

Gene's first book, "The Awakening" was published in March of 2022.